LaTonya Gibson

DRESSED TO KILL

LATONYA GIBSON

UNIQ PUBLISHING, INC.

BALTIMORE, MARYLAND

LaTonya Gibson

DRESSED TO KILL

Copyright © 2013 by LaTonya Gibson

Scripture quotations from the

King James Version of the Bible

All rights reserved. No part of this publication may be reproduced, stored in a retrieval system, or transmitted in any form by means electronic, mechanical, photocopying, recording or otherwise (except for the inclusion of brief quotations in a review) without prior permission in writing from the publisher.

ISBN: 978-0-615-89679-3

Published by
UNIQDESIGN
P.O. Box 41
Owings Mills, MD 21117

FOREWORD

The armor worn by soldiers of antiquity was a priceless commodity. The advantage of armor was complete coverage of the chest (vital organs) while hands were left free to hold a weapon. In biblical accounts and illustrations of King Sennacherib, his success at Lachish was attributed to the type of armor he wore during battle. Though highly beneficial, the armor also had several disadvantages: it hindered movement, its rough exterior caused injuries, and it was expensive to maintain and repair. Additionally, the Canaanite and Philistine control over iron hindered production. Consequently, Israelite soldiers were reduced to the use of animal skins and wood for a short period.

The armor of antiquity was not full proof. Many soldiers whose faith lay heavily upon their iron cast died in battle. In I Kings 22:30-35, King Ahab was struck with an arrow between the scale armor and breast-plate which caused his death. The Egyptian-Thutmose IV was successful in battle as his skilled archer pierced a rival in the armpit of his scale armor. To perfect its use, armor was redesigned to render greater flexibility and protection. Around 1200 B.C. iron swords were refurbished, metal plates or "scales (likened unto fish scales)" were developed and affixed onto leather or cloth rather than animal skin. Decorative helmets, breast plates, greaves or arm guards, gambeson (worn by common soldiers), and the renovated "Coat of Maille" worn by the upper class were available for purchase. Thankfully, our 2013 military men and women can enjoy less complex apparel and more manageable weaponry.

Today's Christian believers are also "dressed to kill" in armor not forged by iron, but by the Word of God! The Apostle Paul's epistle to the saints in Ephesus suggests they clothe themselves in the whole armor of God (Ephesians 6:10-20). Unlike the natural armor that required repair God's spiritual armor will never tarnish nor fail.

II Corinthians 10:36 reveals that our battle is not carnal, but spiritual. We must embrace the Word of God to retrieve His strategic plans for this spiritual battle. I'm excited for the reader who will invest their finance and time to discover keys to maintaining a victorious walk in Christ. This timely book will awaken your spiritual senses and release a new sound. Who am I? God's messenger of peace. Who am I? God's messenger of hope. Who am I? God's soldier anointed, appointed.....Dressed to Kill.

Pastor Linda Harvey
Visionary and Founder,
Fragrance of Faith Ministry, Inc.

INTRODUCTION

There are moments and events that cause us to realize the magnitude of what has been placed inside of us. That moment for me was an opportunity to lead a workshop at The Church of the Redeemed of the Lord in Baltimore, Md. This moment caused me to confront a real truth about me: I'd given in to the habit of concealing my true identity. Occasionally, it was because I hadn't fully investigated what it meant to be me. Consequently, I was unfamiliar with the power associated with being me. At other times I'd hidden my identity while fully aware of the power I possess and simultaneously scared to death of it. I was scared of what it meant to my life. If I accepted this identity I was also accepting the responsibility of it. Yeah, I know it sounds like the ramblings of some fictitious super hero, but the truth ... one that I am not all that anxious to admit even today... is that these are the ramblings of a real life super hero. Me.

As Christians we have each been endowed with some supernatural ability through which we are destined to greatly and magnificently impact the world. We've each heard it before, but are frequently uninterested in admitting it because many of us simply don't believe it. Those of us who do believe it (because we have by chance gotten a glimpse of the power we actually possess) fear being viewed as some freak of nature. The result is that we live like everyone else when we were called to live a supernatural life ... above the world. I know that sounds like lofty church talk, but it is true. We have the ability to live above the dictates, demands, and delusion of society. We just have to be willing to stand out.

There it is – the caveat that many of us are uninterested in satisfying. We simply do not possess the willingness to stand out. Who wants to do that ... purposefully? Each of us will approach this moment from varying degrees of surrender. However, even those who have come to a place of complete surrender have had to (at some point) wrestle with the reality associated with surrendering and can; therefore, relate to the battle that ensues as one comes to the place of surrender.

"Dressed to Kill – Putting on the Whole Armor of God," is about how to effectively utilize our identities as weaponry in the battle of life.

This is a battle with self as much as it is a battle against an external enemy. To equip the believer for this battle, "Dressed to Kill" guides readers through a battle strategy that when implemented ensures victory and progress

I am not just making this stuff up. It is backed up by the word of God and can be traced through scripture. I must admit that when I sat down to prepare this workshop the Lord began to speak to me in a way that I never imagined. The ideas, the scriptures, the method of presentation all seemed to come to me at once. Having had that experience, I was immediately impressed by the unity of scripture and the power of the presence of God. Further, I was challenged by the implications of scripture. But what truly amazed me were the results. When I applied what scripture revealed my life changed.

"Dressed to Kill" provides strategic implementation of scripture through small daily tasks. As you approach this 60 Day Study Guide please consider it as a process and not a quick read. Engage with this study daily. Further, be challenged to purposefully and progressively implement each of the steps as they are revealed.

In the name of Jesus I pray this 60 day Study Guide is as much of a blessing to you as it was to me. Amen.

Ephesians 6:10-18

Finally, my bretheren, be strong in the Lord, and in the power of his might. Put on the whole armour of God, that ye may be able to stand against the wiles of the devil. For we wrestle not against flesh and blood, but against principalities, against powers, against the rulers of darkness of this world, against spiritual wickedness in high places. Wherefore take unto you the whole armour of God, that ye may be able to withstand in the evil day, and having done all, to stand. Stand therefore, having your loins girt about with truth, and having the breastplate of righteousness; and your feet shod with the preparation of the gospel of peace; Above all, taking the shield of faith, wherewith ye shall be able to quench all the fiery darts of the wicked. And take the helmet of salvation, and the sword of the Spirit, which is the word of God: Praying always with all prayer and supplication in the Spirit, and watching thereunto with all persever¬ance and supplication for all saints;

DAY 1

Dressed to Kill

The saying "Dressed to Kill" refers to wearing clothes which are intended to make others take notice. Consider the warfare practices of ancient times. The job of the elite warrior was to standout. After all, a knight in shining armor is not exactly hidden. Instead, he is in plain view for one reason – to draw the enemy out of hiding and, thereby, reveal the enemy's weaknesses and strongholds. It is a daring strategy, but it is a strategy employed by those who confidently approach the battlefield convinced that success is guaranteed. In warfare this is no longer a common practice. Today, a more common warfare tactic is to adorn camouflage – allowing opponents to fit in, and disappear. The goal is to get as close as possible without being noticed. This tactic has its benefits. For one, attacks can be made at a closer range with a more deadly effect. However, there are dangers associated with this method as well. If discovered out, the probability of becoming the captive of the enemy is significantly multiplied.

Unfortunately, the camouflage tactic has spilled into our spiritual lives and we have inadvertently played into the enemy's hand. We camouflage our true identities instead of standing out. Instead of being different, instead of being clearly identifiable as one belonging to God, we blend in. As a result we have put ourselves in danger of becoming an enemy captive.

The truth is if we stand out, we are easily identifiable as opponents to this world's system. We also become easy targets with the responsibility of putting up or shutting up. We don't get to be knights on the battlefield of life and not back up the talk associated with being Dressed to Kill. Here is where many potential knights talk themselves out of showing up to the battle. "If I do this, I'm a target. If I do this and what I thought was my secret weapon turns out to be ineffective, then I am a sitting duck." We ponder these thoughts and immediately crush our own confidence and sap our own strength.

We use a number of excuses to justify our choice to camouflage. "We simply don't want to 'inflict' our views on anyone else." "We don't want to offend anyone." "Camouflage is less intimidating." "Blending in is more fun."

When we make a stand for God, our decision will draw attention to us. Some of us have had the experience of "taking a stand for God" and simply became sick and tired of our every action being criticized and analyzed. We knew we weren't perfect, but it suddenly became everyone else's job to point out our imperfections. As a result, many of us have decided to live "silently saved." In other words, we made a decision to serve God because we know it is the right decision for us; however, we certainly are not going to make any effort to draw attention to our decision.

Simply put, we've decided that being different is not really necessary; it's just too inconvenient. After years of being antagonized, we've decided that blending in has to be better. Safely camouflaged to look just like the world, there is no need to fear being targeted. Yet from this place of "safety", we wonder why Christianity is not as prominent or revered. Simultaneously, we wonder why the miracles and power of God once associated with Christianity appear to be missing from the church of today.

Camouflage is not the uniform of the believer. Unfortunately, this is the attire we've grown accustomed to and seem to prefer. As a result God's glorious church appears to be hidden.

"Ye lust, and have not: ye kill, and desire to have, and cannot obtain: ye fight and war, yet ye have not, because ye ask not. Ye ask, and receive not because ye ask amiss, that ye may consume it upon your lusts. Ye adulterers and adulteresses, know ye not that the friendship of the

world is enmity with God? Whosoever therefore will be a friend of the world is the enemy of God" (James 4:2-4).

We are not experiencing the greatness that the Lord has for us because we are camouflaged. We look too much like our enemy and have become its friend instead of its foe. Our light isn't shining because we are not dressed to appropriately reflect God's glory. It's time to stand out. It's time to Dress to Kill.

God has better for us and, through this study, we are going to acquire better.

DAY 2

How to Approach the Battlefield

As Christians we can approach the battlefield of life confidently knowing that we are guaranteed to win.

Read Ephesians 6:10 and write what it says in the space provided:

_____
_____
_____
_____
_____

How does this scripture boost your confidence as you approach your particular battle?

_____
_____
_____
_____
_____
_____

LaTonya Gibson

Read James 4:7 and write what it says in the space provided:

_____

_____

_____

_____

_____

_____

_____

_____

DRESSED TO KILL

How does this scripture boost your confidence as you approach your particular battle?

_____

_____

_____

_____

_____

_____

_____

How do these two verses relate?

_____

_____

_____

_____

_____

_____

_____

_____

LaTonya Gibson

What additional questions do you have concerning these two verses?

_____

_____

_____

_____

_____

_____

_____

DAY 3 — Recap:

Ephesians 6:10 says, *"Finally, my brethren, be strong in the Lord, and in the power of his might."* This scripture lets us know that the strength we need is found in God. His might is infinite and if we have it, we have access to all we need to overcome any obstacle. The question that stands out to me is how do I stand strong in the Lord? What does that even mean?

James 4:7 says, *"Submit yourselves therefore to God. Resist the devil, and he will flee from you."* This is another confidence booster. We have the ability to put the devil on the run. However, this ability comes with MORE stipulations. We must submit to God and resist the devil. What does it really mean to submit to God? What does resisting the devil look like?

On the surface it appears that this is a no win situation for the believer. However, if we look a little deeper we will see how one verse answers the other. Combining these two scriptures provides us with a formula for success. We can achieve strength in the Lord by submitting to God and resisting the devil. These two stipulations will cause the devil to flee. With his back turned in flight, the devil and his army are vulnerable to ultimate defeat and destruction.
Be assured that our enemy is not as fierce as we've been tricked into believing. He is deceptive and deceitful, but the Bible declares that at some point in history, *"they that see thee (satan) shall narrowly look upon thee, and consider thee, saying, Is this the man that made the earth to tremble, that did shake kingdoms; That made the world a wilderness, and destroyed the cities thereof; that opened not the house of his prisoners?"* (Isaiah 14:16-17). In other words we will look at him and wonder why we were so afraid. What is certain is that he does not care about the well-being of those he destroys. His tactics are effective only because we do not apply the principles of scripture that would cause his every plan to fail. If we want to see the enemy flee, we must get strong in the Lord, submit to the only

one who can guarantee our win and (in our refusal to camouflage and fit in) we must resist.

Ephesians 6:10 and James 4:7 provide the divisions for this 60 Day Study Guide: Be Strong in the Lord, Submit to God, and Resist. As we travel through this study we will uncover how to apply each principle and live "Dressed to Kill."

Section One

BE STRONG IN THE LORD

DAY 4

Know your Enemy

Take the time to list every person you consider to be an enemy. (Be Honest)

_____

_____

_____

_____

_____

_____

The truth is we don't view satan as our only enemy. There are some people who have earned the title. However, as deplorable as they have been, they are not our true enemy. They are actually quite beneficial to our lives.

Take time now to identify why you consider them an enemy. What did they do?

_____

_____

_____

_____

_____

_____

Read Matthew 5:44 and write what it says in the space provided.

_____
_____
_____
_____
_____
_____
_____

Take a moment to politely pray for each of them.

DAY 5

Put it in Perspective

Our enemies are enormous blessings as we prepare for the battle of life. Instead of viewing the people who test us as necessary to our growth and development we find comfort in holding on to their error. Unfortunately, when we do this we fall for the "wiles" of the devil. Ephesians 6:11 says, *"Put on the whole armour of God, that ye may be able to stand against the wiles of the devil."* The wiles of the devil are his subtle tricks designed to annoy the saints or provoke them to spiritual wickedness (Matthew Henry's Commentary). If we are so wrapped up in what a person has done to wrong us, we will fall for these subtle tricks and find ourselves behaving badly. Check each one you've found yourself doing as a result of someone mistreating you:

1. Giving the side eye

2. Lying

3. Fighting

4. Plotting revenge

5. Exaggerating the facts of the story

6. Participating in a plot

7. Keeping the story going

Read Proverbs 6:16-19 and write what it says in the space provided.

_____

_____

_____

_____

_____

_____

_____

_____

Match the seven items listed in Proverbs 6:16-19 with the seven items listed above.

DRESSED TO KILL

Throughout the day be conscious of your behavior and how you express your disapproval of others and their actions. Remember, these are subtle tricks and, by focusing solely on how a person has wronged us, we end up behaving in a way that God not only dislikes, but hates.

What do you do to things you hate?

_____
_____
_____
_____
_____
_____

What do you think God's reaction is to things He hates?

_____
_____
_____
_____
_____
_____

How does the knowledge that God hates these behaviors affect your actions?

_____

_____

_____

_____

_____

_____

_____

_____

_____

DAY 6

Reprobation

The things God hates he destroys. It is not this catastrophic, sky opening destruction that we imagine. Because of His love for us, destruction is subtle and slow. I know that seems torturous, but it is just the opposite. It is grace. In other words, God's method of dealing with our failure provides us with time and opportunity to (1) figure out we are doing something contrary to God's will for our lives, (2) decide we want God's will instead of our own, and (3) repent. Thank God for Grace.

However, when we are fully knowledgeable of His desire for our lives, yet refuse to shift our behavior a different option is made available to us.

Read Romans 1:32 and write what is says in the space provided.

_____

_____

_____

_____

_____

When we know what God desires for us, but get to a place when we enjoy the behavior more than we love God we are in danger of reprobation. We are in danger of inviting the wrath of God into our lives. Here is where the picture gets a little fuzzy because each of us can list three or thirty-three people we know who are living however they want to live. They know what the word says and they are still doing whatever they want to do. They don't seem in danger of anything. In fact they seem perfectly fine. Nothing catastrophic has happened to them, and death doesn't seem to be hunting them down any more than anyone else we know. In fact, we would even go as far as to describe these people as . . . happy.

Read Romans 1:28 and write what is says in the space provided.

_____

_____

_____

_____

_____

_____

_____

_____

God's act of giving one over to something is slow. At the moment of reprobation, the ground doesn't open up and we are not cast straight into hell. Instead, day by day and moment by moment one is slowly given over to and consumed of sin. In other words the thing that is seemingly making that individual so happy is simultaneously sucking the life out of them. We've seen extreme examples of it with persons who are addicted, especially functioning addicts. They are using this "drug" to function. In fact, they've convinced themselves that the drug is needed to function when in fact it is slowly causing them to implode. The same is true of any sin.

Can you identify a sin in your life that is or has the capability of slowly consuming you? What would consumption by this sin look like?

_____

_____

_____

_____

_____

_____

_____

_____

DAY 7

Refuse to be an Enemy Captive

The bottom line is that these subtle tricks of the enemy place us in situations where we have to make decisions to behave in a way that pleases God or in a way that God hates. Annoyed and provoked by the actions of others, we are greatly tempted to give back what is given and inadvertently become a captive of the enemy as he uses what he knows God hates to ensnare us with our own (mis)behavior. To ensure that we make the right decisions when faced with such provocation we have to accept the actions of provocateurs as somehow valuable to us. That's a tall demand of even the holiest of individuals. It is opposite of all of our natural tendencies.

How do we accept them as beneficial to our growth and development?

Read James 4:1 and write what is says in the space provided.

_____
_____
_____
_____
_____
_____
_____
_____

Though it may appear to emanate from some external source, much of the difficulty we encounter is internal. This scripture refers to the war inside of us between wanting to please the Lord and wanting to satisfy our own lusts. Paul said it this way, *"I find then a law, when I would do good, evil is present with me"* (Romans 7:21). "With me" is the temptation to react in an ungodly fashion. "With me" is the ugliness of character that would cause me to respond inappropriately. It's "with me" and will probably be "with me" for most of my life. However, some of the ugliest experiences in life have beautifying effects. In fact, one purpose for the difficulty we face in life is to change parts of us which are resistant to change. To get the most out of this truth, it is essential to know the purpose of each situation, submit to the process and adopt the character trait the situation is attempting to build in us.

DAY 8

It Is Actually Working for My Good

Read Romans 8:28-29 and write what is says in the space provided.

_____
_____
_____
_____
_____
_____
_____

The lesson embedded in these two verses is that God uses all things to work together for our good and that good is defined as our transformation to the likeness of Christ. He is attempting to beautify our character with his own.

List the characteristics of Jesus.

_____
_____
_____
_____
_____

Now take the time to connect the situation/person once considered an enemy to the characteristic of Jesus they are working in you.

_____

_____

_____

_____

We should approach every situation looking for the good – how this situation is beautifying our character to make us more like Christ. Once we identify the good we must apply the appropriate actions, thereby, effectively causing that good to become a permanent part of us. In this way we adopt more and more of God's character. The more of His character we adopt the more we start to resemble "His Son". The more we resemble Jesus, the more we reflect God's glory in this dark world. Simply put, this type of change will get us noticed. It will cause us to stand out like a knight in shining armor. When we start to stand out, then our true enemy will reveal himself.

Take a few moments to write a thank you letter to one of your enemies. Be specific about how he/she has helped you become more like Christ.

_____

_____

_____

_____

_____

_____

DAY 9

An Offensive Strategy

Because we are no longer attempting to defend ourselves against people, we are able to change our stance from defensive to offensive. The enemy's strategy has been revealed, the true purpose of the hurt has been identified, and our true enemy has been uncovered all because we dared to stand out. Now our defenses are fortified against the enemy of our souls and we can focus on how to bring the fight to the devil. Forget running in fear, trying to avoid being targeted. If we are going to show up in the middle of an open field dressed in shining armor, running simply is no longer an option. We're showing up to fight. We can show up confidently because we know something the enemy isn't expecting us to figure out – The fight is fixed.

Read James 4:7 and write what it says in the space provided.

_____

_____

_____

_____

_____

_____

_____

_____

How does scripture prove that the fight is fixed?

_____
_____
_____
_____
_____
_____
_____
_____

If we do two things our victory is guaranteed: submit to God and resist the devil. These two things cause the devil to turn tail and run.

_____
_____
_____
_____
_____
_____
_____
_____

Section 2

SUBMIT TO GOD

DAY 10

Submit To God

Read Ephesians 6:12 and write what it says in the space provided.

_____
_____
_____
_____
_____
_____

Define the following terms:

a. Principalities :
_____
_____
_____
_____

b. Powers
_____
_____
_____
_____

c. Rulers of darkness of this world

_____
_____
_____
_____
_____

d. Spiritual wickedness in high places

_____
_____
_____
_____
_____

Until we've encountered these things, we haven't encountered our true enemy. Every other situation is simply equipping us for the real fight. They are making us strong in the Lord, and in the Power of His might.

Each of these entities is a force of darkness. Their job is to ensure everything in their "jurisdiction" is dark. The stronger you become in the Lord the more you reflect God's glory. God's glory is light that overpowers darkness!

Read 2 Corinthians 4:6 and write what it says in the space provided.

_____
_____
_____
_____

All light is a reflection of God's glory. We only know God's glory through the character of Christ.

Utilize 1 Corinthians 13:4-7 to describe Christ's character.

_____

_____

_____

_____

_____

_____

_____

In submitting to God what areas of your character need adjustment?

_____

_____

_____

_____

_____

_____

_____

As we continue to submit these areas of our lives to God, Christ shines through us. As a result we stand out and get noticed – the very definition of being Dressed to Kill. We are literally in Shining armor. Now it becomes essential for us to check our armor and ensure we are properly prepared for what's next.

DAY 11

Keep Your Armor Clean

As previously stated, dressing for spiritual warfare is counter intuitive. We are not looking to camouflage ourselves. Camouflage requires we either hide in the bushes or wallow in the mud.

Hiding entails being among and with. Read 2 Corinthians 6:17 and write what it says in the space provided.

_____
_____
_____
_____
_____

We are not called to be among or with, but to be separate. Sure this is not always the easiest road to travel, but it's the road which guarantees the presence of God. His presence gives us access to His direction and insight. Conversely, when we are surrounded by others, the sound of the masses has the ability to drown out the still small voice of God.

Further, we are not called to wallow in the mud of life. Read Psalm 69 and, in the space provided, summarize how the Psalmist defines the mud of life.

When we wallow in the mud of life we allow ourselves to be overwhelmed by the perspectives of other people. God has always focused on redeeming man back to Himself. Sure, we make mistakes and we let God down. We disappoint Him and we fail. It happens. However, the Psalmist points out in verse 5 of chapter 69 that God knows our foolishness and our sins. They are not hidden from Him, yet He willingly forgives and redeems. He restores and brings us back to our place of blessing. We must refuse to roll around in our mistakes. Instead, let's repent and obtain forgiveness from God so that if we get dirty, God can (and will) completely cleanse us. Additionally, we must forgive those who accuse us, forgive ourselves for our mistakes, and move forward in God. Rehearsing our mistakes and dwelling on another's perspective of/comments about our mistakes is mud keeping us stuck in yesterday. Let's get out of the mud.

Day 12

Shedding the Camouflage

Read Ephesians 6:1-10 and write what it says in the space provided:

_____
_____
_____
_____
_____
_____
_____

At the beginning of the 6th chapter of Ephesians, we find a list of things we ought to do to live successful lives. Children should obey & honor their parents, parents should not provoke their children, servants should work for their masters as unto the Lord, and masters should treat their servants fairly. Each of these actions came with the promise of blessing.

After all of that, Paul says no matter what category you find yourself in, you are going to have to be strong. Further, it is going to take more than human strength to live like this. It is going to take strength obtained from being in the Lord. Only "in the Lord" do we truly understand what it means to yield to the instruction and guidance of God. In that yielded state we acquire the might or potency needed to overcome. You see the power is not in the actions, but in how those actions affect those who are able to witness and be challenged by those actions.

Simply put, this type of behavior changes people and has a more powerful impact than anything preached or taught. Therefore, this type of behavior will be opposed. There will always be some reason why living like this is inconvenient. There may be a parent who doesn't deserve to be honored, a child who is willful and only hears when provoked. There may be a boss who is unrealistic and an employee who is disgruntled.

The reasons for not living in adherence to Ephesians 6:1-10 are bountiful and we all have them. List yours below.

_____

_____

_____

_____

_____

_____

_____

_____

_____

_____

Now that we've given our reasons for why we could have difficulty aligning ourselves to Ephesians 6:1-10, match the benefits with the actions:

1. Obeying and Honoring Parents   A. Receive Good from God
2. Not provoking Children   B. Live Well & Live Long
3. Working Hard for a Boss   C. Your Master is Watching
4. Respecting an Employee   D. Nurtured Children who Admire the Lord

What does each of these benefits mean to your own life?

_____
_____
_____
_____
_____
_____
_____
_____
_____

This type of behavior strips us of our camouflage and gets us noticed. Though we may feel exposed and vulnerable, there are benefits. Those benefits ensure we experience a superior quality of life.

DAY 13

Take a Stand

Knowledge of the benefits associated with this behavior is not always enough to take on the disregard that seems to come with it. There will be times when we feel disrespected and taken advantage of. There will be times when we simply do not want to be the person who stands out. The good guy doesn't always win and who wants to be on the losing end of doing what's right? There is nothing fair about that. What do we do when we've done all of the right things, but don't appear to be reaping the benefits? What do we do when we've removed the camouflage and exposed ourselves only to find ourselves being used as target practice?

Read Ephesians 6:13 and write what it says in the space provided.

_____
_____
_____
_____
_____
_____
_____
_____
_____

This verse seems to anticipate the questions we have asked above. When we find ourselves feeling like sitting ducks being used as target practice by some sadistic wretch of a person or situation, the easiest thing to do would be to camouflage ourselves to look (behave) just like our opponents and go in for the kill or respond with circumstantially appropriate rage and attempt to annihilate the situation. However, each of those intuitions are contrary to what God instructs us to do. Verse 13 carefully outlines our response. First, we anticipate the difficulty coming as a result of our determination not to respond according to what others deem appropriate. Secondly, and in anticipation of difficulty, we dress ourselves in the armor of God. Finally, we stand. But note: the only way to stand successfully is if we first get properly dressed.

DAY 14

Let's do what it takes to stand!
LET'S GET DRESSED!

Getting dressed is something we do often. Some of us do it more than once per day. On particularly busy days, we may find ourselves dressing three or four times. The same is often true in dressing for battle; especially if we are dressing for spiritual warfare. Remember we are not camouflaged, needing to be still and silent. We are out in the open for the purpose of drawing attention. Believe it or not, we are daily equipped and dressed to participate in this type of warfare. Sometimes we are dressed multiple times per day.

To get the metaphor, consider this. The knight who wears the armor is incapable of dressing himself. The armor is too heavy and cumbersome and; therefore, the knight needs assistance getting dressed. Do you remember those persons/situations we listed as enemies earlier? We identified their job as those who prepare us for battle by helping us build spiritual muscle. There are a few on that list who we encounter every day. They are functioning as our adjutants. They were strategically placed in our lives to help us get dressed. What about the reasons we gave for not adhering to Ephesians 6:1-10? Do you remember those? They are a type of battlefield and provide the opportunities needed for us to stand out.

We've already identified the behavior that would strip us of our camouflage. If we feel vulnerable it is because we were stripped of what is familiar and we are exposed. However, our God would not leave us defenseless and at the whim of our enemy. God has a defense strategy for us designed to give us the upper hand and ensures our victory. His strategy requires us to be strategically dressed.

Over the next few weeks, we are going to take the time to analyze the situations we face and; thereby, capitalize on them as opportunities to engage in the biblical strategy of warfare. Understand; our commitment to this process will create opportunity. Therefore, some of this will not be fun. In fact, it may be quite challenging, but if we actively engage in each step we will find ourselves appropriately dressed and actively engaged in God's defense strategy. Therefore, be determined not to quit. Take a moment now to ask God to strengthen you through this process and help you endure until the end.

_____

_____

_____

_____

_____

_____

_____

_____

_____

_____

_____

_____

_____

_____

_____

_____

_____

DAYS 15 – 21

THE BELT:

"Stand therefore, having your loins girt about with truth," (Ephesians 6:14a).

Recount the last time you were challenged by the decision to be honest or to tell a lie.

_____

_____

_____

_____

_____

In the scripture "loins" refer to the reproductive organs. We are well aware of how one lie gives birth to another. Sometimes telling the truth is challenging, but when we give into the temptation of lying we give life to a fictitious version of reality. After a while, we find ourselves surrounded by little lies rapidly morphing into life consuming fallacies. Great amounts of time are dedicated to protecting these fallacies. After all, if the lie is revealed, our identity changes and we are labeled liar: untrustworthy, deceiver, trickster, fraud. That sounds (and looks) a lot like the devil. It is one of the ways we find ourselves donning camouflage.

Conversely, when we speak the truth, truth is reproduced. We can live a life in the freedom of knowing there is nothing for us to cover up. There is nothing to remember in an effort to ensure we always tell the same story. When we tell the truth, People may not always like what we have to say, but they will have to admit we always tell the truth. We obtain labels such as trustworthy, honest, reliable, and dependable. It's the beginning of standing out and it is a decision made every day . . . . . multiple times a day.

Further, truth not only refers to honesty, but to the only absolute truth there is – the Word of God. In our everyday conversation we discuss truth as we see it. Our realities, shaped by our experiences, vary from person to person. However, the absolute truth of God's word never changes. Instead of purely speaking from our limited perspectives it would greatly benefit us and those with whom we interact if we adopted the habit of speaking the truth of God's word. His word pertains to every aspect of life and when discussed daily challenges us to reproduce godly character and behavior.

Challenge Instructions for days 15-21:

There are two challenges for this week. Once you read challenge one skip to challenge two and complete both throughout the course of the week. Start each day reciting Ephesians 6:4a.

Challenge 1:

Most say it takes 21 days to form a habit. For the next 21 days commit to only speaking the truth. However, for the sake of this study take the next seven days to consciously and purposefully speak the truth. There may be times you want to refrain from saying anything at all, but refuse to lie. At the end of each day take a few moments to journal the results.

Day 15

_____

_____

_____

_____

Day 16

Day 17

Day 18

Day 19

Day 20

_____

Day 21

_____

Challenge 2:

For the next seven days, look for opportunities to interject God's word into conversations. At the end of each day take a few moments to journal the results. What changed about your conversations? What demand did this place on you?

Day 15

_____

Day 16

Day 17

Day 18

Day 19

Day 20

Day 21

DAYS 22 – 28

THE BREASTPLATE:

"and having the breastplate of righteousness;" (Ephesians 6:14b).

Romans 3:22-23 says, *"Even the righteousness of God which is by faith of Jesus Christ unto all and upon all them that believe: for there is no difference: for all have sinned, and come short of the glory of God."*

This scripture reveals that righteousness is not equivalent to sinless. Instead it is synonymous with faith in Jesus as Christ. What does it mean to you for Jesus to be Christ?

_____

_____

_____

_____

_____

_____

_____

_____

_____

_____

The breastplate covers our vital organs – the organs that are essential to life. The breastplate of righteousness is an essential piece of our defense. Without it we are vulnerable to experiencing spiritual death because the most vital element of our Christian experience is left unprotected.

Romans 3:22-23 says, *"Even the righteousness of God which is by faith in Jesus Christ unto all and upon all them that believe: for there is no difference: for all have sinned, and come short of the glory of God."* This means that our righteousness is not just about living according to a set of rules. It is about living with the belief that Jesus actually did die in our stead. Jesus actually took on our guilt and our punishment in order for us to experience a life at peace with God.

Our behavior is influenced by what we believe. Because we believe that Jesus is the Christ there are some things that we just won't do. It has nothing to do with how holy we are, but has everything to do with how grateful we are for what He has done. We are so grateful to Him for dying on our behalf that we can't bear the thought of doing anything that would minimize His sacrifice or in any way disrespect His suffering.

Further, His ultimate act of love gave us access to heavenly things. As the Israelites anticipated the coming of the Messiah, they also anticipated a time in which the Kingdom of God would be established in the earth with an eternal earthly king. When we believe that Jesus is Christ we also believe that His kingdom has come. He is the eternal ruler of that kingdom and, as joint heirs with Christ; we have access to all He demonstrated rule over – healing, prosperity, deliverance, etc. His lordship puts us back in the place of dominion. It makes us the head and not the tail, above only and never below. Thus our behavior is shaped by the knowledge that we have gained access to heavenly things through our faith in Jesus as Christ..

How often do we consider our faith in Jesus as the Christ (the chosen one) when making major decisions? How often do we consider Christ's sacrificial work on the cross before making major decisions? How often does our gratitude for His sacrifice influence our decision making? How often does our knowledge that we have access to heavenly things influence how we go about acquiring earthly things? If we did it more, we could avoid a lot of unnecessary heartache and stress.

Take the time to write a short "Thank You" note to Jesus for His sacrificial work on the cross.

_____

_____

_____

_____

_____

_____

_____

_____

Challenge Instructions for days 22-28:

There are two challenges for this week. Once you read challenge three skip to challenge four and complete both throughout the course of the week. Start each day reciting Ephesians 6:14b and Romans 3:22-23.

Challenge 3:

Consider the last few decisions you've made. If you considered your faith in Jesus as the Christ (the chosen one) prior to making any of those decisions, would it have changed how those decisions were made? Would it have changed the decision? Would the results be different?

_____

_____

_____

_____

Challenge 4:

What are some of your pending decisions? What impact does your faith in Jesus as the Christ have on your decision? It is tempting, but refuse to give in to the idea that Jesus "has nothing to do with this." If we were honest, we would recognize that His presence in our lives affects everything. Note your conclusions here.

_____

_____

_____

_____

_____

_____

_____

_____

_____

_____

_____

_____

_____

_____

_____

_____

_____

DAYS 29 – 35

THE SHOES:

"and your feet shod with the preparation of the gospel of peace;" (Ephesians 6:15).

How has your life changed since you accepted Jesus as your savior?

_____
_____
_____
_____
_____
_____
_____

What would you tell a person who asked you why he/she should believe in Jesus?

_____
_____
_____
_____
_____
_____
_____
_____
_____

When we begin to view our daily situations as opportunities to apply truth and righteousness (the belief that Jesus is the Christ) to our lives, something dynamic takes place. Dressed in this fashion we draw attention. The change becomes so noticeable and those around us want to know the source of this change. 1 Peter 3:15 says, "But sanctify the Lord God in your hearts: and be ready always to give an answer to every man that asketh you a reason of the hope that is in you with meekness and fear:" According to this scripture we should always be ready to give an answer. We should always be prepared to tell people about the source of our change. However, we have to be careful not to become arrogant about the change that has taken place in us. Becoming puffed up will push people away instead of drawing them. Simply remember, the change has only taken place because we have chosen to activate our faith in Christ and apply that faith holistically to our lives. Therefore, remain meek before the Lord.

In addition to meekness, the scripture tells us to give an answer in fear. This is not telling us to be scared, but to expect to be challenged. Respect the fact that once we make this open proclamation, our goodness will be challenged. 1 Peter 3:16 says, *"Having a good conscience; that, whereas they speak evil of you, as of evildoers, they may be ashamed that falsely accuse your good conversation in Christ."* In some instances people will speak of us as if we were doing wrong. It will upset those who are used to the old version of us. However, we must remember not to fault those who have a difficult time dealing with it. He/she is merely doing his/her job of sharpening us by providing us an opportunity to examine our growth and share our faith.

The enemy of our souls is the one who's actually upset. Our difference has provided us with an opportunity to tell someone about Jesus. Our standing out has caused him to lose another one. As a result of our difference the enemy will rear his head. Our good character will draw him out and we may suffer for it. But be encouraged. 1 Peter 3:17 says, *"For it is better, if the will of God be so, that ye suffer for well doing, than for evil doing."*

Challenge Instructions for days 29-35:

There are two challenges for this week. Once you read challenge five skip to challenge six and complete both throughout the course of the week. Start each day reciting Ephesians 6:15 and 1 Peter 3:15.

Challenge 5:

Throughout this week look for opportunities to tell people about how your life has changed since you've come to know Jesus as your Savior. When the opportunities arise, make the most of them. How did you capitalize on opportunities to share Christ this week? What opportunities did you miss? How could you have made better use of that moment? What did you learn from the experience?

_____

_____

_____

_____

_____

_____

_____

_____

_____

_____

_____

_____

_____

_____

Challenge 6:

How has your change been challenged? Commit to responding with meekness and gratitude. For each way you've been challenged identify a benefit to being challenged in that way?

_____

_____

_____

_____

_____

_____

_____

_____

Section 3

RESIST THE DEVIL

DAYS 36 – 42

The Shield of Faith

We've submitted to the Lord and as a result we're walking through life adorned with bright shiny armor. The battle strategy has worked. The enemy has noticed us and is slowly being drawn out. We're standing in the middle of the battlefield. Now we must take heart and know most assuredly that we are not left defenseless.

"Above all, taking the shield of faith, wherewith ye shall be able to quench all the fiery darts of the wicked" Ephesians 6:16.

What are the promises of the Lord concerning your life?
___
___
___
___
___
___

The Lord has made certain promises concerning you. The enemy knows those promises because they are in direct contradiction to the curse that has been placed on his life. Genesis 3:15 says, *"I will put enmity between thee and the woman, and between thy seed and her seed; it shall bruise thy head, and thou shalt bruise his heel."* This is ultimately speaking of Jesus; therefore, when we align with Jesus' ultimate work (accepting Him as Christ) and begin to function in God's plan for our lives we too bruise the enemy's head. He's taking body shots, but our aim is for his head. A body void of a head has no ability to function.

The enemy's sole focus is to shoot us down before we have an opportunity to behead him, or remove his headship from our lives and the lives of those connected to us. He's taking body shots because we are of no use to him dead; however, alive and malfunctioning we can be used to negatively impact the kingdom of God. According to Ephesians 6:16, the enemy's weapon of choice is the dart. The "fiery darts of the wicked" are mainly composed of disbelief. First, he wants us to disbelieve what God has stated concerning us. This is his first tactic because he understands that humans are mostly self centered. If he can convince us that salvation is in no way beneficial to us, he's gotten a good footing in our lives and in the lives of those connected to us.

As evident by his statements to Eve in the Garden of Eden (Genesis 3), the enemy does this very subtlety, usually utilizing half truths. Thus it is important that we familiarize ourselves with what the Lord actually says concerning who we are, our rights and privileges in Him, and our eternal access to heavenly things.

Challenge 7

Each day over the next seven days write down one scripture with promise. Take some time to write down what that promise means to your life. Refuse to doubt it and look for it to come to pass in your life. Make each scripture with promise your daily affirmation by meditating on it throughout the day.

Jeremiah 29:11

_____

_____

_____

Matthew 11:28-29

Isaiah 40:29-31

Philippians 4:19

Romans 8:37-39

John 14:27

_____
_____
_____
_____
_____
_____

2 Corinthians 5:17

_____
_____
_____

This week is over and you have spent the entire week reflecting on just a few of the promises God has made you in His word. You have access to the greatness of God and the fullness of His power. He has made yet another promise in Isaiah 40:8. What does this promise mean to you? How does this promise affect the others you've read throughout the course of the week? What impact does this promise have on any trials you may be facing at this time or may face in the future? Why is this knowledge effective in resisting the devil?

_____
_____
_____
_____
_____

DAYS 43 – 49

The Helmet of Salvation

"And take the helmet of salvation," (Ephesians 6:17a).

What is the "formula" for salvation?

_____

_____

_____

_____

_____

_____

_____

Helmets protect our heads. The helmet of salvation protects our thought life. What if we filtered our thoughts through the plan of salvation? Consider this: the Bible says, *"That if thou shalt confess with thy mouth the Lord Jesus, and shalt believe in thine heart that God hath raised him from the dead, thou shalt be saved"* (Romans 10:9). What would happen if we filtered our thoughts through the confession that Jesus is Lord? Lord means that He's ruler, king, and the absolute final authority. What would happen if we filtered our thoughts through the belief that God raised Him from the dead? If God can raise Jesus from the dead, can't he raise a dead situation? If God made death have positive results, can't positive things come out of negative situations?

This type of thinking renders the enemy powerless. The helmet of salvation, when worn appropriately, makes it impossible for us to be taken out by our own view of what is and what is not possible. The finished work of Christ makes EVERYTHING possible. Jesus says so in Mark 10:27, *"And Jesus looking upon them saith, with men it is impossible, but not with God; for all things are possible with God."* Because of the finished work of Christ we can be sure and certain of our power over the impossible. We realize that impossibility is really opportunity. As a result we don't give up simply because we THINK something is too hard. We don't give up because others say it's too hard. We simply don't give up.

Challenge 8:

Throughout this week remind yourself that Jesus is Lord in the midst of each challenge you face. Because He is Lord, He has the final say. Next remind yourself that God raised Him from the dead. Then ask yourself what is impossible. Consider the opportunities instead of the impossibilities associated with this challenge. Journal about your experience.

_____

_____

_____

_____

_____

_____

_____

_____

_____

_____

DAYS 50 – 56

The Sword of the Spirit

"and the sword of the Spirit, which is the word of God:" (Ephesians 6:17b).

Refer to the list of challenges you have faced last week. How did reminding yourself that Jesus is Lord affect your perspective of those challenges?

_____

_____

_____

_____

_____

_____

"The thing that hath been, it is that which shall be; and that which is done is that which shall be done: and there is no new thing under the sun" (Ecclesiastes 1:9). There is nothing that happens in your life or mine that catches the Lord off guard. In fact, an answer for every question and direction for every crossroad can be found in scripture. It is not always the answer we want, but there is an answer. When we wield the sword of the Word of God, the enemy only has one response – he flees. He may be able to stand against us, but he cannot stand against the Word of God.

"In the beginning was the Word, and the Word was with God, and the Word was God . . . And the Word Became flesh, and dwelt among us, (and we beheld his glory, the glory as of the only begotten of the Father,) full of grace and truth (John 1:1, 14). He cannot stand

against Jesus. Remember, we know that Jesus is Christ – He has given us access to heavenly things. Through God's word we operate by the laws of a kingdom from which the devil was evicted. Further, we've come to know Jesus as Lord. He has the final say. His final word on all matters pertaining to believers is that everything has to work together for our good.

Challenge 9:

Take the previous list of challenges and match them to scripture. Apply the answer provided for you in scripture and journal the results. What does the answer require of you? What good is revealed about the issue you're facing? How does this affect your attitude toward the situations?

_____
_____
_____
_____
_____
_____
_____
_____
_____
_____
_____
_____

DAYS 56 – 60

Conclusion

Submit yourselves therefore to God. Resist the devil, and he will flee from you – James 4:7

Armored according to Ephesians 6:10-17, our lives become enemy resistant. However, we must first have a clear understanding of who our real enemy is. It is not our nosey neighbors or our jealous co-workers. We have to stop wasting so much of our time and energy attempting to fight them. They are probably the best thing that has ever happened to us. They either have the job of helping us to build spiritual muscle or they are preparing us for real warfare by equipping us with everything we need to experience success. The longer we focus on them, the less time we have to live a life dedicated to causing the enemy to flee. Take the next four days to do something kind for the people who have been less than kind to you. After all, their actions have only made you stronger.

Remember: Dressing in the whole armor of God is not a onetime thing. Daily we must apply these principles. As a result we'll experience a lifetime of results.

Submit: Apply truth, righteousness, and spread the gospel.

Resist: Have faith in the word, allow salvation to govern your thoughts, and utilize the word of God as a practical answer to all of life's questions

Watch the devil flee.

www.ingramcontent.com/pod-product-compliance
Lightning Source LLC
Chambersburg PA
CBHW060428050426
42449CB00009B/2184